West Point
THE LIFE OF A CADET

West Point
THE LIFE OF A CADET

A picture story by
JACK ENGEMAN

New Revised Edition

Foreword by General W. C. WESTMORELAND, United States Army

Lothrop, Lee & Shepard Co., Inc.
NEW YORK

Other books by Jack Engeman

Annapolis: THE LIFE OF A MIDSHIPMAN
U.S. Air Force Academy: THE LIFE OF A CADET
The Coast Guard Academy: THE LIFE OF A CADET
Doctor: HIS TRAINING AND PRACTICE
The Catholic Priest: HIS TRAINING AND MINISTRY
Airline Stewardess
College: THE LIFE OF A STUDENT
Student Nurse

CONTENTS

ACKNOWLEDGMENTS

I wish to thank the Superintendent of the United States Military Academy at West Point, the Commandant of Cadets, the Dean of the Academic Board and staffs for their cooperation in the preparation of this book.

Special thanks go to Major Richard L. Hargrove, Infantry, Major Fox McCarthy, Infantry, and Major Richard C. Bennett, Corps of Engineers, for their invaluable assistance and advice.

I would also like to thank the many officers, cadets and enlisted men who so generously gave of their time and cooperation.

It was a source of great pleasure to work with that fine body of young men who make up the Corps of Cadets, and I thank them all for being such good-humored, understanding and patient models.

JACK ENGEMAN

West Point, N.Y./May, 1967

FOREWORD

Through the years thousands of America's finest young men have marched across the plain at West Point and into the future as commissioned officers in the armed forces of the United States. They have faced great challenges bravely. Their contributions to the security and progress of the nation have been unsurpassed.

In time of increasing specialization elsewhere, the military profession is becoming more diverse and more demanding. The challenges of today are expanding across the spectrum of human endeavor. To serve his country adequately in his chosen profession, the military officer must be more than a leader and an administrator. He must be able to apply the principles of economics, psychology, sociology and political science. But above all he must be a military man, thoroughly versed in the skills and techniques of his profession.

Duty requires the same selfless devotion it always has. Honor requires personal standards that do not change. But our country today requires each military officer to have deeper knowledge, broader understanding and greater military competence.

That the men who go forth from West Point will rise to this ever-widening challenge, I have no doubt.

W. C. WESTMORELAND
General, United States Army

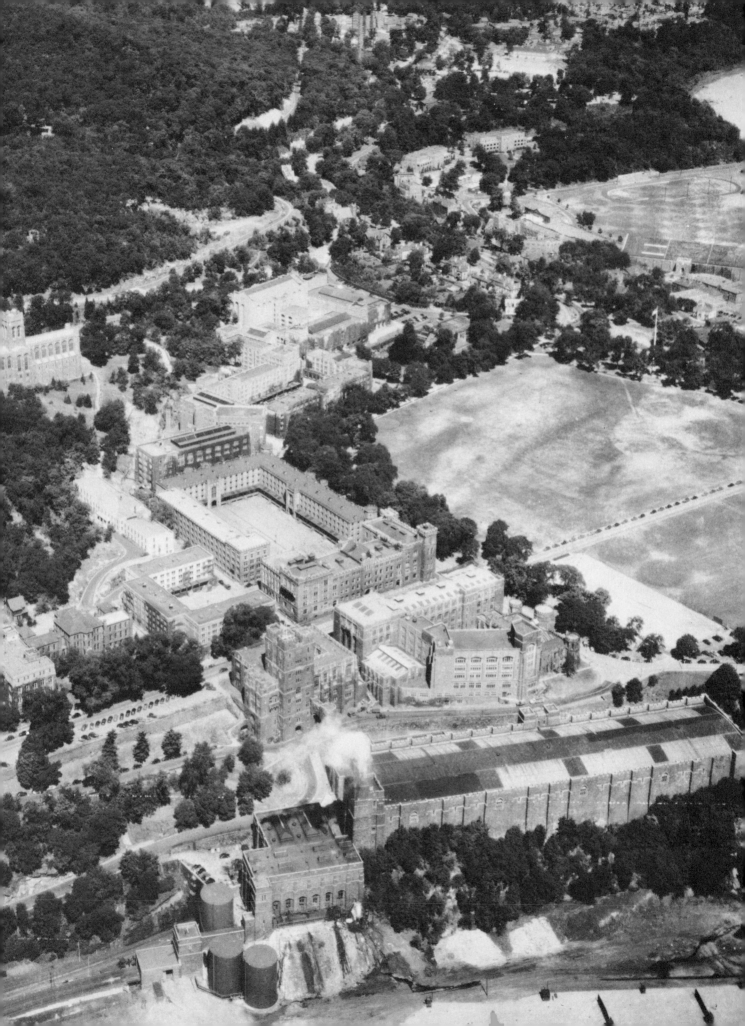

THE MISSION OF THE UNITED STATES MILITARY ACADEMY

The mission of the United States Military Academy is to instruct and train the Corps of Cadets so that each graduate will have the qualities and attributes essential to his progressive and continued development throughout a career as an officer of the Regular Army.

Inherent in this mission are the following objectives:

To provide a broad collegiate education in the arts and sciences leading to the Bachelor of Science degree.

To develop in the cadet a high sense of duty and the attributes of character with emphasis on integrity, discipline and motivation essential to the profession of arms.

To develop in the cadet those physical attributes essential to a career as an officer of the Regular Army.

To provide a broad military education rather than individual proficiency in the technical duties of junior officers. Such proficiency is, of necessity, a gradual development, the responsibility for which devolves upon the graduates themselves and upon the commands and schools to which they are assigned after being commissioned.

New Cadet Barracks

This first two-month orientation period, beginning in July, is called New Cadet Barracks. Its purpose is to give the new cadet, or plebe, the necessary basic military training, indoctrination and motivation to enable him to take his place in the Corps of Cadets.

There are about thirteen hundred new cadets each year who have become candidates for admission through presidential or congressional appointments or from the enlisted ranks of the Regular and Reserve Army.

The new cadet is between seventeen and twenty-two, and has successfully passed the necessary academic, medical and physical requirements. He is now a member of the Regular Army and as such receives more than $150 per month pay, plus a ration allowance for his food. His pay is sufficient for his necessary uniforms, textbooks, equipment, and incidental expenses, with sufficient money left over each month to go into a fund for his officer's uniform. Excellent medical, dental and hospital services are furnished without cost.

Intensive drills, hikes and athletic competition under the guidance of First and Second Classmen and officers of the Department of Tactics make this the most Spartan and rigorous period (popularly known as Beast Barracks) in the life of a cadet and it may be said to be the time in which the "men are separated from the boys."

New arrivals

Waiting in line to be measured for uniforms

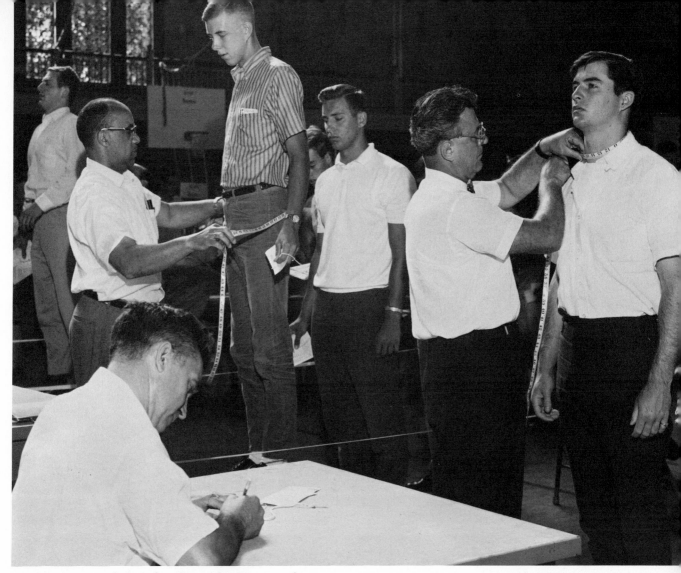

Being measured for the first of many uniforms

Regulation
haircut

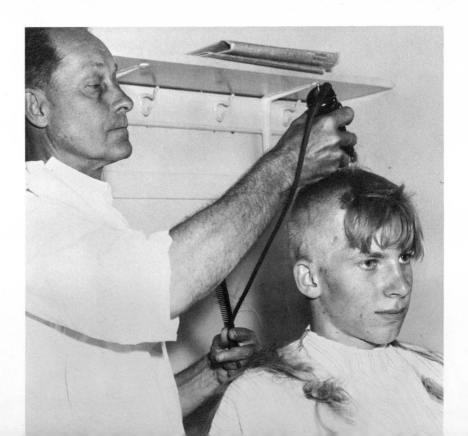

13

New cadet
receiving instruction
from member of
New Cadet (Beast)
Barracks detail

Learning to "Dress-left"

Hat should be comfortable

Shoes must fit perfectly

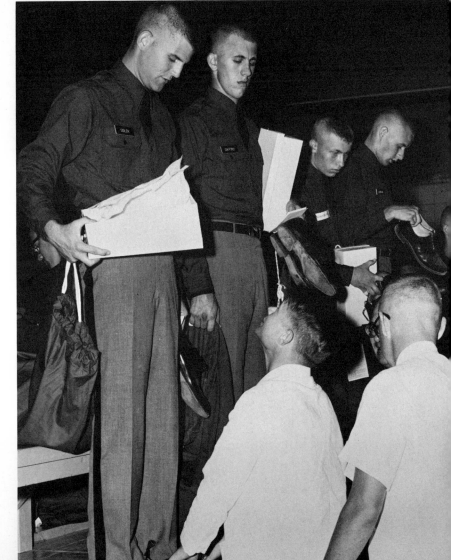

First day's issue includes shirts, underwear, bathrobe, shoe-shine kit, towels and laundry bags

New cadets being sworn in

Conditioning drills

Bayonet exercises

FIRST PARADE

Company tactical officer inspecting new cadets in ranks before first parade

After weeks of practice, the first parade

CONDITIONING MARCH

New cadets returning from a conditioning march

FULL FIELD INSPECTION ON PLAIN

Upper classmen instructing Fourth Classmen (Plebes) in putting up tents

Inspection by tactical officer
and New Cadet detail

Commandant and Commanding Officer
New Cadet Barracks check daily status report

A company street
with full field equipment displayed

Boy watchers

PLEBE HIKE

Plebes on the march

New cadet battalion observes
live fire demonstration

Eating C rations during noon break in hike

Shaving cream over everything

BIVOUAC AT LAKE FREDERICK

Preparing for inspection

Catching up on the news
during a rest period

24

Swimming area

A musical interlude

Letter home

Refreshment

PLEBE-PARENTS WEEKEND

Tactical officer and his wife greet cadet's family at reception during Parent's Weekend

Cadet shows younger brother and nephew around the Academy

Parents observe a demonstration of physical fitness

Special parade for parents

Life in Barracks

The living quarters of the Corps of Cadets, consisting of the Central Barracks, the North Barracks and the old and new South Barracks, are under the supervision of the Commandant of Cadets and the officers of the Department of Tactics. The company tactical officers work in close contact with the cadets and by precept and example, counsel and guidance, correction and—when required—disciplinary action, guide the development of proper military and personal habits.

The barracks accommodate about four thousand cadets in two-man and three-man rooms. Shower and toilet facilities are on each floor. The barrack complex also contains the headquarters of the Commandant of Cadets and the offices of the various regimental, battalion and company tactical officers. The class clubrooms provide billiards, table tennis, and television.

The rooms in the Central Barracks once occupied by now-famous generals, such as John J. Pershing and Douglas MacArthur, are still occupied by cadets.

Three men of the same class share a room

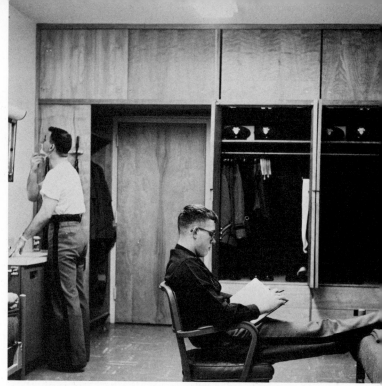

Rooms are sparsely but comfortably furnished

Cadets must keep their rooms clean at all times

Latest electronic devices are available

It isn't all study

A uniform for every
purpose

WASHINGTON HALL

Entire Brigade is served at one time

Fifteen thousand meals
are served each day

Plenty of food with second
helpings available

THE CADET MESS

Seats!

Attention to orders!

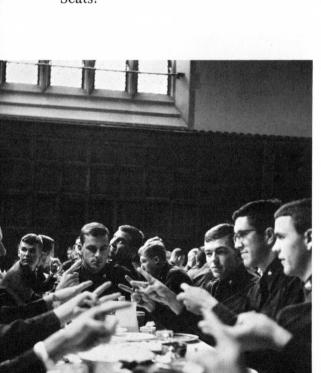

Matching out for extra dessert

A discussion of the Civil War

CENTRAL AREA

Noon formation

Reading orders

Synchronizing watches

Grades are posted weekly

Walking wounded

Shooting the breeze

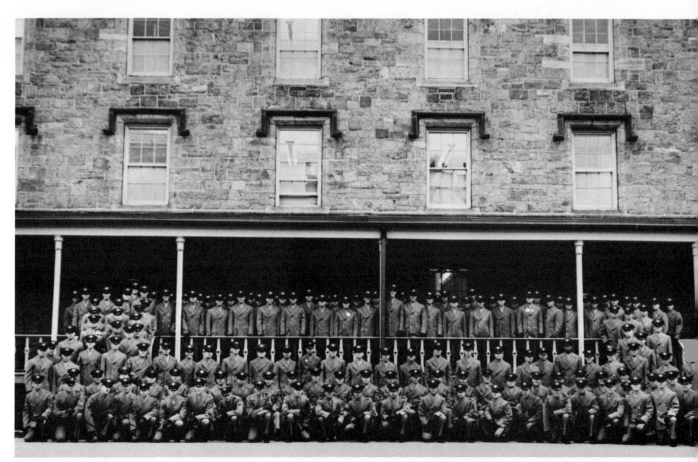

Former Eagle Scouts

DUTY

The Commandant of Cadets

Commandant with Cadet Brigade Staff

Central Guardroom

Cadet Officer of the Day and Officer in Charge

Officer of the Guard and Army officer

Upper classman correcting a plebe

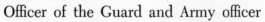

Posting the "Corps Squad" lists

Flags designate the uniform changes for each day

Walking the area is an extra duty

Changing the guard

Sorting the mail

Mail call

All's quiet during evening study hour in Central Barracks. A cadet
Officer of the Guard stands in the east sallyport

EXCHANGE WEEKEND

For a number of weekends during the academic year the Second Classmen participate in exchange programs with the other service academies: the U. S. Naval Academy, the U. S. Air Force Academy, the U. S. Coast Guard Academy, and the U. S. Merchant Marine Academy. Students from the other academies live, eat, study, and relax with the cadets. West Point Second Classmen replace their opposite numbers at the various academies. In this way a better understanding between the future officers of the armed forces is promoted.

During Exchange Weekend midshipmen from the Naval Academy are classroom observers. This is a Saturday morning social sciences class

West Point cadets meet their midshipman
guests from Annapolis

Roommates for a weekend

Midshipmen meet Army mascots
at athletic meet

Arguing the merits of their own Academy

PREPARATION FOR PARADE

A plebe minute caller gives count-down before formation for parade

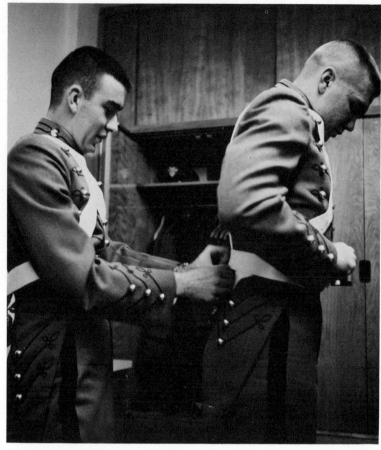

Helping hand

Tactical officer inspects his company

Last minute check

Right shoulder arms!

At rest

Fall parade

Spring parade

Summer parade

CADET STORE

Smoking is allowed

Civvies can be worn on leave

There are places to ski on the reservation

Part of his monthly allowance is used to purchase supplies

Music for his record player

CHAPEL

Interdenominational services are held in the Cadet Chapel. Historic American Army flags hang overhead

Marching to chapel

Ushers

MEDICAL AND DENTAL CARE

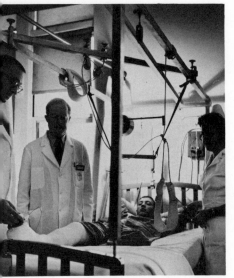

Excellent medical care
is provided

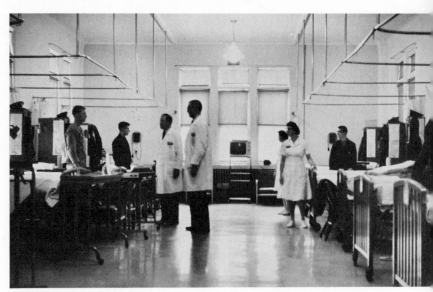

The hospital is fully staffed and equipped

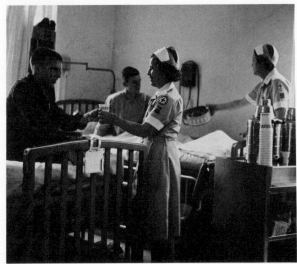

Gray Ladies make their rounds

Recuperating

Physiotherapy

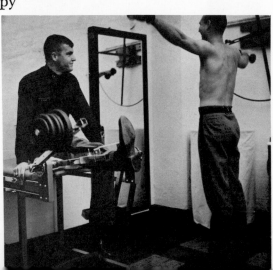

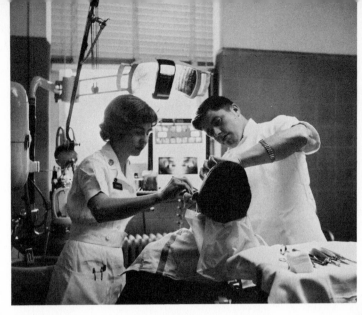

Cadets are given the best of dental care

The most modern equipment is used

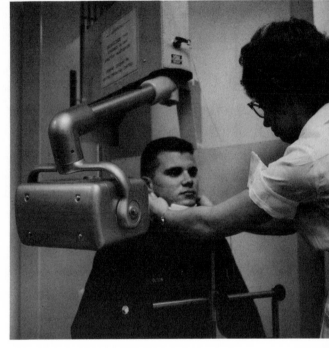

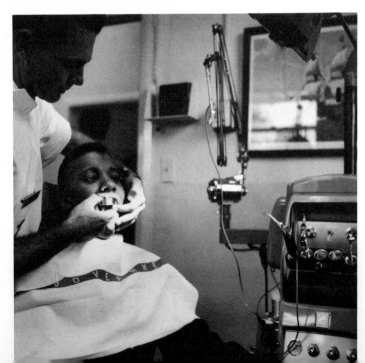

Each cadet is provided with a tooth guard for protection in sports

49

Academic Year

The United States Military Academy prepares selected young men for service to their country as professional officers of the United States Army. The total curriculum is designed to develop those qualities of character, intellect and physical competence needed by the officer who is prepared to lead the smallest combat unit or to advise the highest government council. The program includes the sciences, the humanities and military and physical training and leads to a Bachelor of Science degree upon graduation. It forms a basis both for graduate education and for further professional development.

In the academic curriculum, standard courses provide the essential core of knowledge of mathematics, science, engineering, the social sciences and the humanities and an understanding of the application of this knowledge to the solution of problems. Advanced and elective courses afford the opportunity to develop intellectual capacities and to concentrate in areas of particular interest.

THE CURRICULUM

SUBJECT	CLASS
Mathematics	PLEBE
Engineering Fundamentals	(first year)
Environment	
English	
Foreign Language (Chinese, French, German, Portuguese, Russian or Spanish)	
Mathematics	YEARLING
Chemistry	(second year)
Physics	
Foreign Language	
History of Europe and America	
English/Psychology	
Fluid Mechanics/Thermodynamics	SECOND CLASS
Electric Circuits/Electronics	(third year)
Atomic and Nuclear Physics/Engineering Mechanics	
Economics/U.S. Government	
Law	
2 Elective Courses	
Civil Engineering	FIRST CLASS
History of the Military Art	(fourth year)
Contemporary Foreign Governments: Europe and Asia/ International Relations	
Ordnance Engineering	
Leadership/English	
2 Elective Courses	
Tactics	ALL CLASSES
Physical Education	

GOING TO CLASS

EARTH, SPACE
AND GRAPHIC SCIENCE

A problem in graphical representation

A problem in engineering drawing

CADET OPEN TIME
RULES

1. Cadets have priority.

2. First come, First served.

3. RUN TIME ≤ 5 minutes/problem

GENERAL ELECTRIC

Every cadet receives instruction in
computers

CHEMISTRY

Measure accurately

Weigh the sample

Heat slowly

Check results

A classroom demonstration

Individual lab instruction

LANGUAGES

Individual work in the language laboratory

The instructor looks on

Replay and check

Russian

Chinese

German

Portuguese, French and Spanish are also taught

ENGLISH

Preparing an outline for an English theme

English seminar in the library

Note-taking

A classroom conference

Recalling a visit to London

Instructor observes a writing project

COMPUTER CENTER

The Computer Center serves
all academic departments

A cadet prepares his own run

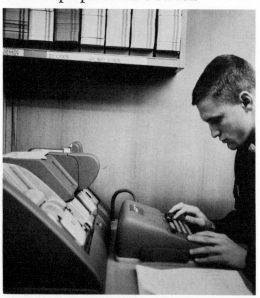

Checking a printout

Discussing related equipment

Remote outlet in classroom

ORDNANCE

Wiring an analogue computer

Checking the diagram

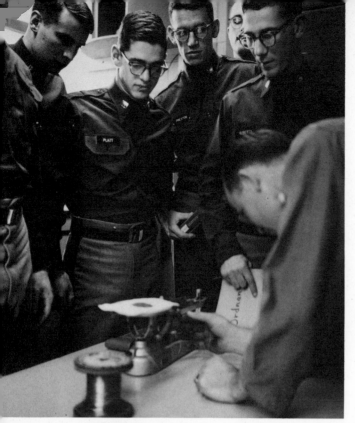

Weighing the rocket fuel

Examining the rocket nozzle

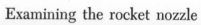

Preparing to fire

MILITARY ART
AND ENGINEERING

Checking a design problem

Lessons from a campaign

Officers from other services (in this case a naval officer) also instruct

Discussing bridge components

Soil mechanics

PHYSICS

The subcritical reactor

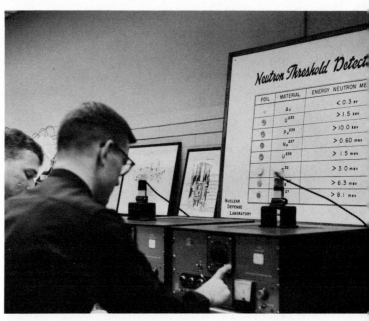

Using monitoring equipment

Direction of force

The slide rule solution

A classroom
demonstration

Class in optics

Discussion period

Problems in nuclear physics

$$\varphi(r) = \frac{3Q}{4\pi\lambda_{tr}} \times \frac{e}{r}$$

$$L_{Be} = 20.8\ cm, \quad \lambda_{tr} = 1.43\ cm$$

$$\varphi(10) = \frac{3 \times 10^9\ n/sec}{4\pi(1.43)\ cm} \times \frac{e}{10}$$

$$\varphi(10) = .115 \times$$

MATHEMATICS

Checking his work

Showing the solution

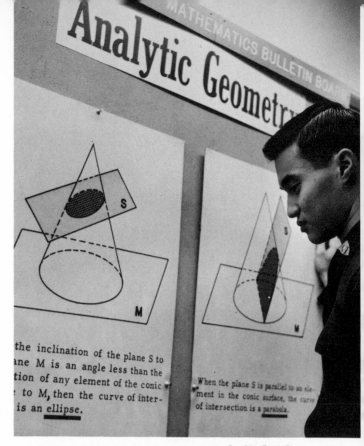

The instructor checks cadet's solution

A hall display

Working at the boards

ELECTRICITY

Correcting a problem

Wiring and testing a circuit

Analyzing a circuit

Discussing the solution

Board work in electricity

The instructor checks solutions

Lab work at the cadet desks

LAW

First Classman checks
steps in buying a car

Discussing the elements
of proof

SOCIAL SCIENCE

A Round-table Discussion

MECHANICS

Instructor explains lab equipment

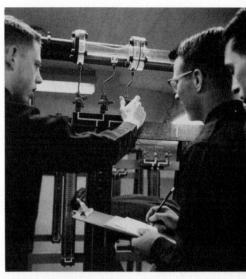

Fluids experiment

Checking data

Making the run

Collecting data

Discussing the experiment

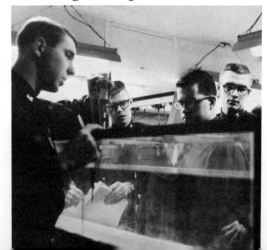

ELECTIVES

Cadet receives advice on selecting electives from a counselor in the Office of the Dean

Cadets seek professional advice from an instructor

LIBRARY

Reference Room

Using microfilm projector
in Periodical Room

Improving reading speed

The Library contains 250,000 volumes

Hometown news

Rare-book collection

West Point Room

MILITARY LEADERSHIP SEMINAR

Coffee with the Superintendent

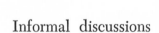

Informal discussions

The Commandant shares
his experiences

Department of Physical Education

Physical education programs are designed to increase muscular strength, power, endurance, fundamental coordination, balance and flexibility; to enhance mental health and efficiency; and to develop the personal requisites necessary for military effectiveness and leadership.

The physical training program requires that each cadet take an annual physical performance examination, run an obstacle course against time and participate as a member of his company team in a different intramural sport each season, unless he is currently a member of a varsity team. Rivalry is keen for the Corps championship; fair play and teamwork are stressed.

General of the Army Douglas MacArthur, a former Superintendent, summed up the spirit of the program: "On the fields of friendly strife are sown the seeds that in other days, on other fields, will reap the fruits of victory."

Boxing

Wrestling

Survival swimming

Swimming

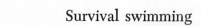

OBSTACLE COURSE

All cadets must pass this yearly test

INTRAMURAL SPORTS

Soccer

Football

Track

Swimming

INTERCOLLEGIATE SPORTS

Distraction from the game

Cheering section

Soccer

Cross-country

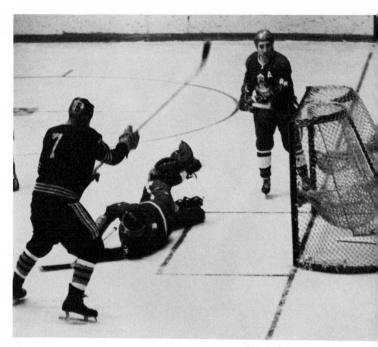

Ice hockey

Basketball

Baseball

Lacrosse

ARMY-NAVY GAME

"Ladies and gentlemen, the United States Corps of Cadets!"

"Roll that score way up!"

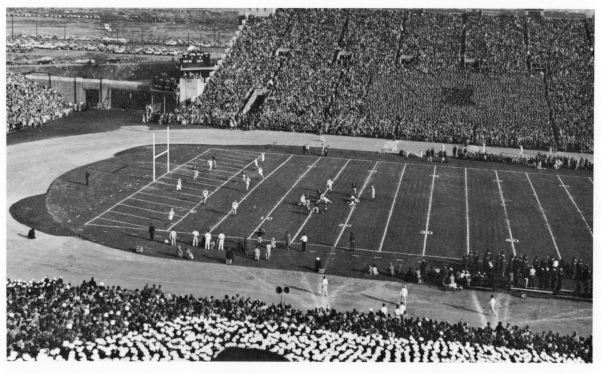

Another touchdown!

Making arrangements for
after the game

Recreation and Extracurricular Activities

As a relief from study and parades, a cadet enjoys a full social life of hops (dances) every Saturday night, movies on Saturday, Sunday and holidays, swimming, canoeing, sailing and picnicking at Delafield Pond and Lake Popolopen in the summer and ice skating and skiing in the winter.

There is a wide variety of extracurricular activities. In music, there are such groups as the Glee Club, Choir and Cadet Band. In journalism, a cadet can work on the staff of *the Howitzer, The Pointer or Bugle Notes,* or be a cadet press and public information representative. In dramatics, the One Hundredth Night Show is written, produced, and acted by cadets. Other clubs include Foreign Language, Sailing, Chess, Ski, Skeet, Amateur Radio, Scuba, Rugby, Karate, the Debate Council and Sport Parachute.

GRANT HALL

Drags (dates) arriving for weekend activities and hop

Cadets meet their guests in Grant Hall

Cadet hostesses

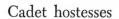

Drags leaving after weekend

85

Portraits of famous Army officers such as General of the Army Dwight
D. Eisenhower hang in Grant Hall

WEAPONS ROOM

The room contains a snack bar, tables, jukebox and dance floor and is open weekends for dragging

"BOODLERS"

These are snack bars in Cadet Facilities

LEE HALL

This is a recreation room for upper classmen and their drags

Cullum Memorial Hall for plebes

On the way to the First Class Club

AN INFORMAL HOP

A FORMAL HOP

EXTRACURRICULAR

Howitzer photo lab

Sailing Club

Skeet Club

Radio disc jockeys at Station KDET

Astronomy Club

Chess Club

Ski Club

Fencing Club

Karate Club

SCUBA Club

Sport Parachute Club

West Point is proud of its famous Glee Club

Cadet Chapel Choir

Plebe Glee Club

Folk song group

SUNDAY SCHOOL

Cadets teach the post children

Historic Spots

Medal of Honor

Patton Monument

West Point Museum

Fort Clinton

Trophy Point

Thayer Monument

Fort Putnam provides a romantic setting

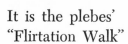
It is the plebes'
"Flirtation Walk"

A chance to be alone

A beautiful view of the Hudson River Valley

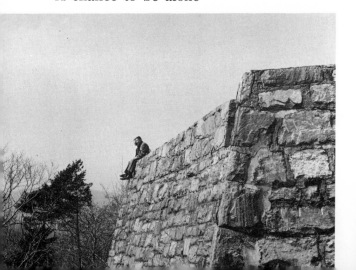

June Week

June Week means "recognition" to the plebe and his acceptance as an upper classman by the Corps, with a thirty-day leave thrown in for good measure. The Yearling and Second Classmen also are looking forward to their added privileges and responsibilities, to say nothing of their thirty-day leaves. To the First Classman, however, it is Graduation at last and a commission in the United States Army. For all, it is a festive week of parades, dragging, picnics, garden parties and canoeing and swimming, culminating in the colorful Graduation Parade, Graduation Hop and Graduation!

Reviewing line of graduating cadets

Plebe recognition

GRADUATION

A diploma and congratulations from the Vice President of the United States

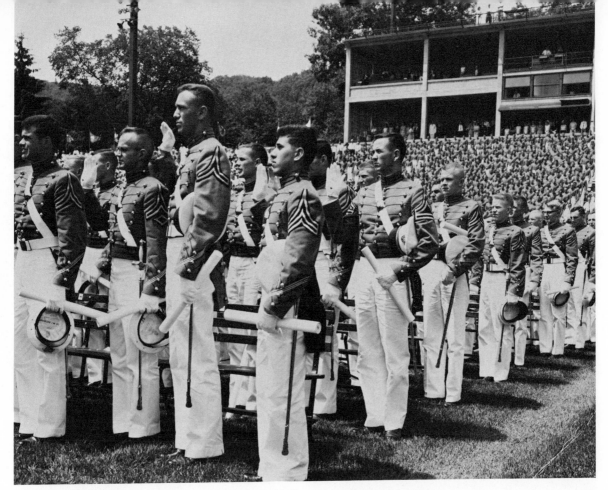

Being sworn in as second lieutenants in the United States Army

Officers at last!

GRADUATION HOP

Camp Buckner

During July and August, the entire Third Class and part of the First Class go to Camp Buckner, a military reservation near West Point, for summer training. The camp is staffed with veteran officers and enlisted men who are well qualified to give instruction in the art of warfare as practiced by the Infantry, Armor, Artillery, Engineers and Signal Corps. The use of weapons is taught along with the tactical training of small combat units.

Relaxation is provided by summer sports, and hops are held on Wednesday and Saturday nights in Barth Hall.

Constructing a concertina fence

Equipment training

Instruction on the 81 mm. mortar

Laying the 81 mm. mortar

Putting a round in the tube

Firing

M-60 machine gun

Field communication equipment

Airmobile operation

During Mine Warfare Training, a cadet who accidentally sets off a mine or booby trap gets his name on a cross in the cemetery

Fire direction

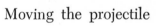

Moving the projectile

Loading

Orienting the weapon

Fire!

An instructor explains the construction of an aluminum footbridge

Platoon races against time to complete construction

Platoon must now cross

Platoon leader is dunked

Observing operation of an Armored Vehicle
Launched Bridge

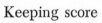

Light antitank weapon

Keeping score

Firing line

There is relaxation and fun on weekends

BUCKNER STAKES

The Buckner Stakes caps the military training for the Third Class summer. It consists of a series of practical exercises in which the cadets demonstrate their proficiency in all major subject areas taught during the summer. Cadets go through this eight-hour test by platoon groups, double-timing between stations of the test. At the end of the day, the scores are determined and the winning platoon is rewarded with a long weekend pass.

Running the
obstacle course

Map reading

Mortar problem

Computing artillery data

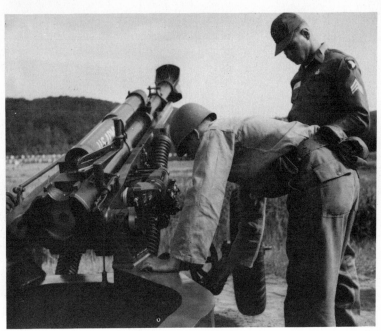

Laying the 105 mm. howitzer

Emplacing an antitank mine

Camp Commander and staff select the winning platoon

CAMP ILLUMINATION WEEKEND

This is the final social whirl of the Camp Buckner summer. It consists of an awards review, an awards luncheon and a cadet stage play satirizing the humorous events of the summer. There are informal dances on the beach and in Barth Hall. There is a parade of floats, a beauty contest, sky-diving demonstrations and an outdoor barbecue. The weekend ends with a formal hop in Barth Hall.

Sun and fun
on the beach

Watching sky diving

Patio and porch of Barth Hall

Drags can change at Harriet Rogers House

Food is supplied by Cadet Mess for cookouts and picnics

Preparing floats

Parade formation

One of the many benefits of being
a West Point cadet

Competitors
for title of
Camp
Illumination
Queen

The Queen

Entrance Requirements

Admission to the United States Military Academy can be gained only through nomination from one of the sources authorized by law. Members of Congress and various service-connected categories constitute the main sources of nominations.

All candidates must be citizens of the United States except for those authorized from the Republic of the Philippines and the American Republics other than the United States. They must be at least seventeen but not yet twenty-two years of age on July 1 of the year of admission. Also, candidates must never have been married, and must be of good moral character.

The factors used in determining scholastic qualification for admission are previous academic records and performance on specified College Entrance Examination Board tests. These tests must be taken on or before the nomination category test date indicated in the Admissions Section of the current United States Military Academy catalogue. The College Board tests required are: The Scholastic Aptitude Test (verbal and mathematics sections), the English Composition Test, and either level one or level two of the Mathematics Achievement Test.

Each candidate is required to establish his qualification in physical aptitude. Qualification is determined by an examination designed to measure strength, coordination, muscular power, endurance, speed and agility. It is given at military test sites as specified by the Department of the Army. A more detailed discussion of this examination as well as a listing of all the various performance tests included in the Physical Aptitude Examination in the catalogue.

The qualifying medical examinations for admission to the Military Academy are held at authorized Army, Navy and Air Force Medical Centers at times and places designated by the Department of the Army.

Requests for information on admissions and for the United States Military Academy catalogue should be addressed to: The Admissions Office, United States Military Academy, West Point, N. Y., 10996.